fourteen poems

Issue 12

First published in 2023 by Fourteen Publishing.
fourteenpoems.com

Design and typeset by Stromberg Design.
strombergdesign.co.uk

Proofreading and copy editing by Lara Kavanagh.
lk-copy.com

Printed by Print2Demand Ltd, Westoning, Bedfordshire, UK.

ISBN:
978-1-7391697-8-7

Hello.

Welcome to Issue 12 of *fourteen poems*, an anthology of contemporary queer poetry. Whether you're a subscriber, regular reader, or a complete newbie, I hope you'll enjoy these poems and queer stories from across the globe!

As always, I hope we offer something of a snapshot of what it is to be queer today, while simultaneously acknowledging the multitude of voices and ideas from within our community. No community is a monolith, after all.

But I do think there's something that these fourteen poets share: a desire for unfettered connections, whether that be through love, through community, through friendship, or even through dancing.

In some of these poems, our writers are looking for a connection that's free from prejudice; prejudice that might manifest itself in internalised homophobia that we've soaked up after years of micro (and macro) aggressions, or from an external world that often feels like it's built on hate.

Our writers grapple with some of these big issues in their poems; I hope you see something of yourself here too. And if you're struggling to find your own voice, I hope that some of these voices shine a light that helps you find your way.

In this issue, I'm particularly thrilled to see so much crossover with our recently launched *Bi+ Lines: an anthology of contemporary bi+ poets*, with three poets appearing in both books. Our bi+ siblings are so often overlooked in the queer community, and I'm so happy to offer a spotlight across our different collections.

Dive into our latest fourteen poems and remember, we post readings of most of our poems on our Instagram page, so you can put a face to your favourite one. I always find that I get something completely unexpected when I hear the poets read, so do check in. And remember, I love hearing from you.

Email me at hello@14poems.com and tell me about your favourite poem.

Thanks, as always, for the support,

Much love,

Ben Townley-Canning
Editor

Instagram: @14poems
Twitter: @fourteenpoems

contents:

Eric Yip was born and raised in Hong Kong. His poems appear in *The Poetry Review, Magma, The London Magazine, The Adroit Journal,* and *Best New Poets.* He won the 2021 National Poetry Competition and was shortlisted for the 2023 Forward Prize for Best Single Poem - Written. He is working on his first pamphlet which plays with the idea of sight and photography to search through experiences related to queerness, family, dislocation, and memory.

Instagram: @eric.ycw

Twitter/X: @metapheric

Tenor

Now that I feel love, all metaphors
have turned duplicitous. We lied
down in the meadow to read.
Grass crammed into our necks.
There were no buildings, only words
or sequences of words I could use
to describe my feelings for you but
chose to reveal piecemeal so as to
remain mysterious. And when
you laid your calves over mine,
the fuzz reminded me of grass cut
exceedingly finely, or that night
when we shed all pretences, took
off our clothes, split fresh peaches
in the dark and ate them.

Eric Yip

Godelieve de Bree is a Dutch-American poet currently based in London. Her work has been published by TATE and *The Los Angeles Review of Books*. She's a T.S. Eliot Prize Young Critic and was a member of the Roundhouse Collective 22/23.

Twitter/X: @godelievedebree

Brokebutch Mountain

After Danez Smith

I want Ennis to be a long-haired butch
who writes short stories, makes lino prints
of things like coffee brands
& exhausted with city life

has moved to Wyoming
to be a farm hand. I want
Jack to be a stud
who routinely makes butter

from her own song-fed cattle &
who all her life has lived on river land.
I want to watch their diner meet cute
the week after Ennis gets there,

their first kiss
as hesitant as rain. I don't want
any bullshit; no cheating or lying
to their wives, no threats, bruises

or close calls. I want a love story
simple as a shirt on a hanger.
I want a shot of a hand cradling
a shaved head, two beers on a bar,

white sun reflected off
their matching belt buckles,
an unmade double bed, their dog,
Jack's routine of a morning walk

around their ranch while Ennis
sleeps. I don't want to know
how they fuck or make love,

I just want to see them share their lives

like you would a slice of pie & when
Jack dies at the end, frail and grateful,
their time together has been just time,
not an allowance.

Godelieve de Bree

T.S. Leonard is the author of *God Save the Queens!* (Irrelevant Press, 2022) and poems published in *Foglifter, Post Road, Frontera, & Change,* and *The San Franciscan*. Leonard was a finalist for the 2022 Jane Underwood Poetry Prize. Leonard appeared in the multimedia program Spectral Transmissions (Portland Art Museum, 2020), and as a poetry finalist in the 18th Annual Saints + Sinners LGBTQ Literary Festival. Originally from Kansas City, Missouri, he lives and teaches in San Francisco.

Instagram: @tsleonard

A National Anthem

The last time some man called me a faggot, mountains sang:
a bird called America blushed, devoured roses. The thorns
stuck in her teeth, like tough bits of meat. He got in my face.
I did not blink. I sang back to my country, a quilt of torn flags;
his hiss hung around my lips. His breath stank. Dogwoods
bloomed pink above us. My father's father's mother plucked
a folk ballad on catfish bones. The Ozarks wept and bled mud
waterfalls, wagons broke. He said, know what that makes you?
Goddamn unamerican. His snout nearly brushing mine. Dirt
behind his eyes. My country, whose violences I cannot shake—
whose purple pumps through my veins— whose song sticks
in my lungs— whose nasty history of who owns whom is no more
his than mine— then this country, too, is a faggot. He should be
so lucky as to have a name. To have a changing flag and a history
of plague and dancing. A whole prairie shivered. He stood still.
The last time some man called me a faggot, I became a nation.

T.S. Leonard

Kevin Madrigal Galindo is a first generation hijo de su chingada madre from South San Francisco by way of Zapopan, Jalisco, Mexico. His first chapbook, *Hell/a Mexican*, was published by Nomadic Press in 2022 and he has also had work published in *The Boiler, Bozalta,* and *KQED,* among others. He is currently reimagining the world with abuelita wisdom, and trying to channel rage into change.

Instagram: @kmadrigal

Twitter/X: @kmadgalindo

Self portrait as list

self portrait as recipe
self portrait as corrido
self portrait as sex addict
self portrait as queer
self portrait as dry-hopped beer
self portrait as anxiety & fear
self portrait as huevos rancheros
self portrait as boy in his abuela's wedding dress
self portrait as "are you sure he's not gay?"
self portrait as Minnie, the disobedient poodle mutt
self portrait as el fajo coming to whoop my ass
self portrait as pair of shoes stolen through broken glass
self portrait as non-stick frying pan
self portrait as Kevin, the mischievous kid from Home Alone
self portrait as childhood fight for the red Ninja Turtle
self portrait as three freshly picked squash blossoms, now wilting
self portrait as Cognitive Behavioral Therapy
self portrait as faded 2003 Corolla with roll up windows
self portrait as Spongebob edition Kraft mac n' cheese
self portrait as Macuilcozcacuauhtli, the god of gluttony
self portrait as identity crisis
self portrait as waiting to be held
self portrait as temporary spines
self portrait as nopal that grew from concrete, its fruit on the way

Kevin Madrigal Galindo

Dan Fitt-Palmer is a mixed-heritage, bisexual poet from Stoke-on-Trent, UK. His work has appeared in *Magma, Smoke, Hit Points: an anthology of video game poetry* (Broken Sleep Books, 2021), Young Poets Network, *Bi+ Lines: an anthology of contemporary bi+ poets* (fourteen poems, 2023), and *Propel Magazine.*

Handshaker Evangelising

While vacuuming the shrine room,
rolling over the dots of red wax
that have anointed its wide matted landscape,
a spider asks me if I would consider
letting him, and his ash-lace home,
stay undisturbed. I lean in to listen
to his clicking mandibles,
hear percussive stories, unlikely exploits –

My silk is hair
          for horses who pull
                    gods' chariots / I need
                              this many eyes because
                                        I don't trust clouds –
                                                  I had a name before
                                                            the flood, you know /
                                        Eight legs for no reason.
                              You can have one,
                    whatever / Spider-Man is
          my favourite hero, just wish
he wasn't skinny /

He rolls a cigarette like a caught
fruit fly, legs deftly turning it,
vertical spit. He grins, knows
he has won me over as he says

Uncle,
          please don't throw me out /

Dan Fitt-Palmer

Daniel W.K. Lee is a queer, Cantonese American, third-generation refugee poetry hustler born in Kuching, Malaysia. His debut collection of poetry, *Anatomy of Want*, was published by QueerMojo/ Rebel Satori Press (November, 2019). He has been widely published in online and print publications. Daniel lives in New Orleans with his whippet, Camden. Find out more about him at danielwklee.com

Instagram: @strongplum

Twitter/X: @danielsaudade

Facebook: @thedanielwklee

Pomelo

Treason
that our bodies did not
crash into carnality considering
the succulence of your fruit. You
rebuffed my request that you sit on
my face, our sex like sand bags
in hurricane season—needing to be filled
to save us. But waiting can thicken
the pith: the memory of you once
dripping on my tongue now
a pomelo, white mouthfuls
of bittersweetness.

Daniel W. K. Lee

Laura McKee is a poet based in London, UK and has had work published by *Ink, Sweat and Tears* and *Anthropocene Poetry,* among others. Her debut pamphlet *take care of your hooves darling* was published by Against the Grain in 2023.

Instagram: @laura.mckee1

Twitter/X: @lauramckee_fyeh

plum

In the late 18th century, the word plum was used to indicate something desirable

what is the same colour as this   I've seen it reached for by varicose veins   aubergines and
purple sea stars   plum blossoms bloom to become young fruit petals of blossom fall   to
bloom again across pavements   mature fruits may have a dusty white coating   this too is
bloom   wax bloom   to wax to grow   to bloom to flower   a sticky flowering a natural
secretion

this is the lipstick I opted for after trying all the testers on the back of my hand like practice
kisses improper enough   dark enough   witch like in a way   not straight edged hat in
cool goth black not the wicked witch is dead   alive enough to say
fuck the patriarchy   and also may I fuck you please   an overly polite witch

maybe this colour makes me think of other lips   I should own up to this or know this by
now know it like the back of my hand I study the back of my hand   it looks older in winter
my wrinkled finger joints properly known as interphalangeals properly seen now seem to be
cunt lips properly known as labia minora

in botany this fruit is a drupe   outer fleshy parts surround a single shell with a seed inside
indehiscent it does not split at maturity along a line of weakness   it will decay   or be taken
and eaten   before it can open up and release its contents

used for a tart   a sauce   or other reduction   crammed into a jam jar   or cupped fresh to the
mouth it begs to be eaten   attention seeker   exhibitionist   doesn't sit politely in a bowl boasting
of keeping the doctor away   though sometimes it daydreams of being an apple   dunked into water
and floating witchlike   reached for by willing mouths

it lets the curve of itself shine up at you   a gentle but sure bite tears   into the skin that held it
together   let the sweetness run down your chin   and river itself to your neck   down across your
collar bone to your breasts
the mess of it all

Laura McKee

Rasha Abdulhadi is calling on you, dear reader, to join them in refusing and resisting the genocide of the Palestinian people. Wherever you are, whatever sand you can throw on the gears of genocide, do it now. If it's a handful, throw it. If it's a fingernail full, scrape it out and throw. Get in the way. The elimination of the Palestinian people is not inevitable. We can refuse with our every breath and action. We must.

Twitter/X: @rashaabdulhadi

Fathering Lessons

how to swim, shoot, drive, and cook meat rare
how to avoid answering questions about where
you're from and never name the place
your father was born, how to be wide like the ocean
of his name so whole nations can sink inside you,
and no one on the surface ever be wiser. how to
punish with a blistering kindness, to touch a branch
lightly enough to know if it can hold your weight,
to touch people just as carefully. how not to be used
for someone else's plan, and how lack of purpose
is a definite path to landscape suicide.
how a heart, weathered by betrayals,
becomes weaker without something to believe in.

Rasha Abdulhadi

Rona Luo is a queer, neurodivergent poet and acupuncturist based in London, UK. A Kundiman fellow and member of Southbank Centre's New Poets Collective, her work has appeared in *ANMLY, The Massachusetts Review, Mom Egg Review,* and *Bi+ Lines: an anthology of contemporary bi+ poets* (fourteen poems, 2023). In 2023, she was commissioned to produce a visual poem for London's Royal Festival Hall 'A Great Sense of Space' exhibit.

Instagram: @pomelolo

Half Tulip

Odd to be half nose, half tulip   Let me put it this way
I am drawing on the wall   surgery

To say tulip without the other half, well that means
dipping a finger under elastic

Think of an elevator stretching over the Catskills
frozen lakes, red walls, tornado sirens

blasting our streets from unseen speakers
Long rows of clouds like ploughed fields

Then inside   what other

It is tulip too, yet it is formless, held with particles
checking each other   To say assumption or power, no

better to file into the dark elevator
shuffling hard slippers, almost clogs

Or Rihanna reworking that erroneous equation
concerning light   All this has to do with

the half nose, the nose you are being
How they mistook me for straight

You are tulip   One half nose, the other half
nose, then nose to nose

Rona Luo

Ben Dalitz is a queer/dyke poet, artist, and campaigner. Their work has been published in *Bi+ Lines: an anthology of contemporary bi+ poets* (fourteen poems, 2023). When they write and dream queer liberation, they do so in deep solidarity with the people of Palestine.

Instagram: @ben.dalitz

nightlife

oh god for a gay Eden / unable to
tell whether the low ceiling drips
with sweat or whether the sky opens
to a thousand stars / whether these
are open shirts and shoelaces glowing
under UV lights / or vines ascending
huge waxy green leaves catching
purple moonlight / oh god for the
openness of movement / the way we
flow into each other / boys grinding /
dykes kissing / two best friends twirling
joy to the room / the acid pinks and lime
greens, sex like a neon sign / oh god
their drip, the envious arousal of looking /
and the majesty of being watched / oh
god for my cheeks to change to marble
my clothes to flow / oh god for bodies
in water, the summer river at night
is the original bathhouse / oh for the
blooming flower of a deep kiss on my
throat huge opening peony dripping
with an excess of petals / oh for peony
maximalism / oh for my back to the
wall, to the earth / oh god to glow in sin,
oh god / for my cheeks to be neon
billboards of shameless desire / oh god
to fuck in toilets overgrown with stickers
and generous graffiti / someone left their
wisdom here / nights so full, our feet
and hands move to share all we've learnt /
so the little prince, breaking a branch from
the garden of diamonds / golden trees
under the pink green moon / can know
that his dancing was more than a dream

Ben Dalitz

Stephanie Colwell is a writer from Atlanta, USA, now based in Seattle, USA, where she completed an MFA in Prose at the University of Washington. Her work focuses on love and desire through the lenses of Blackness, bisexuality, and big bodies.

Instagram: @steffajae

Eventually (They Wanna Move to Portland)

Can be read with or without elliptical phrases from Harryette Mullen's "Elliptical"

Stop picturing me
pouting in the middle
of some national
park. Radically
imagine me panting
with a smile, or better
yet, indoors. Careful.
So sexy and
emotionally "healthy".
Tell white lies to save
feelings, lick sweat
and wish it wasn't
happening, so on. Set
boundaries, keep
them, so on. Don't get
what it means to be
particular. Had to
been lying because
who is that unaware
of what they want?
Don't make
regrettable jokes, or
talk shit because it's
exhilarating.
Choosing for both of
us. Quitsville. The
righteous don't get
down like that.
Radically imagine me
among the trees, I'm
begging. Say
anything without
taking it back. Toes

while learning to walk.
Be aware lol. Desire
to be an idea and not
a person. Dreaming.
Said it first. Kissed
first too. Life outdoors
involving farmland.
Convenient.
Mostly mirage.[1]

Stephanie Colwell

1 "may we be / more than a snack. may we be less than a balanced breakfast," (Alexis Pauline Gumbs, *Spill*, 137).

Nicholas Wong is a poet, translator, and visual artist writing in his L2 from Hong Kong. He is the author of *Crevasse* (Kaya Press, 2015) and *Besiege Me* (Noemi Press, 2021), and the winner of the Lambda Literary Award for Gay Poetry, He was also a Lambda finalist in 2022. His translation and poems have appeared in *The Georgia Review, Cincinnati Review, Poetry London, The Rialto*, and *Foglifter.*

Instagram: @citiesofsameness

The World's Smallest Window

A line of red
fades in like artist
ink on testing kit,
the world's smallest
window whining
for an unwitting view.
We looked at time
pass. Looking,
in the meantime, at walls,
a tufted rug, a pot
of Mother-in-Laws Tongue
shy away from solidarity
by windowsill.
Neither of us talked,
nor the umber mud.
The air, whimsically dead
for fifteen minutes. I forgot,
to be honest, if we
waited that long, or morally long
enough before
undoing the knots
of our jogging shorts.
Fuck the *T*, tediously
for *test*, & I say *C* for *circumscribed,*
can-go-gentle-on-you.
What life is worth living,
lifting, lessening these days?
Just kiss
antigens. Double kiss the nicer ones,
your fear of wet wipes
that made your lips
blossom like forsythia.
If you've read a book,
you should know the pages
can't resist your flipping.

Nicholas Wong

Nadine El-Enany is a writer living in London. Her poetry has appeared in *Butcher's Dog, Magma, Propel Magazine, 14 Magazine.* Nadine was shortlisted for the 2023 Poetry London Pamphlet Competition and longlisted for the 2023 Rialto Nature and Place Competition and the 2022 Fish Poetry Prize.

Instagram: @nadineelenany

Twitter/X: @nadineelenany

White porcelain button

Behind the radiator,
against the wall,
you found me naked,
covered in dust.

My lips were laced
with spiderwebs.
My skin ancient
paintwork peeling.

You placed me tender
on your tongue
to clean me off
like a calf just born.

Nadine El-Enany

Ami Patel is a queer, diasporic South Asian poet and young adult fiction writer. She is a Pushcart Prize nominee whose poetry is published in various places, including *The West Review, Beloit Poetry Journal,* and *They Rise Like A Wave: An Anthology of Asian American Women Poets.* You can find her online at amipatelwrites.com

Instagram: @amiagogo

Facebook: @amiagogo

Abecedarian for My Napping Nephew

Alone together, I settle us in the old chair, shape the heft of my
body to angle us both for comfort. You nestle like a sloppy
comma on my elbow. Nothing wakes you, not even the rising
din of kitchen cleanup, which morphs into lullaby for your
ears, tiny glowing rounds like the translucent of deep sea
fish. You're only three months old but I see it, your inevitable
growth, how it will lasso itself around you, thick and needy,
heaving you into another year, and another, and another.
I imagine all of the burdens of this twisted world, the bruising
jagged pieces – racism, poverty, pollution – that shape our cruel
kaleidoscope of humanity. And I know your heart will waver
learning the world's horrors: floating plastic, noxious fumes,
mass graves. But there are also sweet strands to clutch, keep
nearby: the full warmth of community love, kisses following
ouchies and scraped knees. The dark eyed junco at the window
puffing with song. How I woke the day you were born to a
quill in my heart scratching a hope-bright line with your name,
resolve to love your softness inking out of me like a squid. Your
synapses are working so hard right now to still your jellied joints,
tender and tired from being here, in this new dimension with us,
underdressed for this gala of humanness. Unprepared for the thick
valences of delight and grief that will ruffle you like a stuffed
wardrobe. Some days it'll be too much. But you'll have me, your
x-tra auntie with an unruly garden to settle you: lemon balm,
yarrow, nettle. For every season, a bloom. I will be here as you
zigzag even deeper into the wondrous meadow of your life.

Ami Patel